EVERYTHING

IS

AN

ILLUSION

by

Bhagavan Sri Ramana Maharshi

Sri Nisargadatta Maharaj

Sri Annamalai Swami

Sri Muruganar

Sri Vasistha

Sri Sankara

Introduction, editing and typesetting
© 2011 The Freedom Religion Press

www.thefreedomreligionpress.com

www.seeseer.com

ISBN-13: 978-0-9829651-0-8

CONTENTS

INTRODUCTION

All of the following are dreamlike illusions:

A.   The World.

B.   The body.

C.   The Universe.

D.   All dimensions.

E.   All events motions and actions.

F.   Time.

Almost all of the words in a dictionary describe dreamlike illusions.

What is helpful about reading these types of quotes is that the more you can realize that everything is an illusion, the better you can ignore everything and turn inward.

Many of the quotes indicate that viewing the world as an illusion is essential for Self Realization. Many of the quotes point out that everything disappears when the Self is Realized.

This book contains all of the quotes in Chapter (Step) Two from the book The Seven Steps to Awakening.

Everything is an Illusion is Book Five in a series of six books called The Self Realization Series.

One purpose of The Self Realization Series is to put just one category of quotes into a small book that has the advantage of making it easier to focus, meditate on, grasp and have insight into just one subject at a time. That makes the approach simple, easier and less complicated. The idea is to stay focused on just one subject until you have received everything you need to receive from that one subject. Most people go on to the next subject without ever having learned to apply to their lives the subject they are studying now. The Self Realization series of books are portable practice manuals aimed at helping sincere seekers of Self Realization master one Key to Self Realization at a time.

SRI RAMANA MAHARSHI
(214 – 250)

214. From your true being as Awareness
alienated and deluded
do not pursue appearances,
deeming them as real.
They are false, since disappear they must.
But your own being as Awareness is real
and cannot cease to be.

215. The world appears distinctly
only in wakefulness and dream
with concepts filled.
In concept-free, all empty sleep,
one sees no world;
so then conceptual
is the world's whole substance.

216. The mind bewildered which mistakes
the body for oneself conceives the transient
world of names and forms, makes it seem
real and lovable, and promptly entraps one
in the strong, illusive bondage of desire.

217. The empirical world
     of jostling names and forms is false
     and has no real existence
     in bright, full Awareness.
     Like a ring of fire formed in the dark
     when one whirls fast
     a glowing joss-stick,
     'tis an illusion, mind-created.

218. One ever-present pure Awareness,
     this alone has true existence.

The world perceived and measured by you
is but illusion, jaundiced yellow,
caused by the ego's concepts false
and treacherous desires.

219. Seen in the light of Self-experience
     all this phenomenal world
     is mere appearance,
     like the sky's deep blueness.
     What the deluded, body-bound ego
     perceives 'out there' is mind-created,
     nothing more.

220. This villainous vast world so false
that cheats and churns the minds of all,
how did it come to be? By nothing else but
by the fault of falling from the Self
instead of clinging firmly to It.

221. The world, like snake in rope,
        thief in a stump, mirage in air,
        has no real existence.
        Seeming to be, mere appearance,
        is its nature.

222. By this world
        That world is concealed.
        And this world is by That concealed.
        Names and forms one sees,
        or else one sees
        pure Being-Awareness-Bliss.

223. The world that hides the Self
        is but a dream.
        When the phenomenal world
        is hidden by the Self's bright light,
        Awareness pure, the Self, abides.

224. The nature of this mind-created
     world, now seen in dream-light dim,
     is truly known only in
     that bright Being-Awareness
     which transcends the mind's illusion.

225. Some assert, "This world before our
eyes lacks permanence, 'tis true.
But it is real while it lasts."
We deny it saying,
"Permanence is a criterion of Reality."

226. Some argue, "Though divisible and
split up into parts, the world we know
so well, how could it be unreal?"
We refute it, saying,
"Wholeness too is a criterion of Reality."

227. The wise can nohow deem as real
     a world divided and destroyed
     by time's wheel.
     Whole, eternal, perfect, ever-shining
     and transcending time and space,
     such is the nature of Reality.

228. The goings-on of the empirical world,
true-seeming and beguiling in the mind's
borrowed light, are nothing but illusions
in the bright light of pure Awareness.

229. Only mad folk perplexed because
they deem the false world to be real find
joy in this illusion. The truly wise find joy
in nothing but Awareness which is Being.

230. What is the Self's
        self-transformation as the world?
        A twist of straw
        appearing as a snake?
        Look hard you see no snake at all.
        There was no transformation,
        no creation, none, no world at all.

231. Did the Self lapse
from its own wholeness as Being, you ask,
"How else did this world come to be?"
It came from ignorance false.
The Self can never suffer any change
at any time.

232. Vast, whole, immutable,
     the Self reflected
     in the mind's distorting mirror
     may appear to move.
     Know that it is the image moving,
     the true Self never moves or changes.

233. How can the dark,
     delusive sense of separateness
     affect the Self which is non-dual?
     It is the mind's divisive vision
     which sees difference.
     Awareness knows no separateness
     at all.

234. Those who forget the harm
     the false world there before us does,
     and cling to it
     as real and comfortable,
     mistake, alas,
     a floating bear for a boat
     only to be crushed and drowned
     in the sea of birth.

235. When will the fool who thinks
the body and the world are permanent
and clings to them, find peace?
Only when this folly leaves him
and he trusts and like a limpet clings
to that, the Self within. Thenceforward
he shall never more know pain.

236. Only by courtesy
        is the body,
        vulnerable and born to die,
        called an entity substantial.
        The sole reality,
        the only thing permanent
        and ultimate, is Self-awareness,
        That alone.

237. Know that these countless things
        are pictures in a dream
        and none is real
        apart from the beholder.
        Shun this phantom world
        of names and forms and dwell in
        the pure, blissful being of Awareness.

238. O worldly folk
who long for and run after
an endless series
of unenduring things,
'tis wisdom true to seek and know
That one thing on knowing which
all other things will cease to be.

239. When the full identity is reached that
the Self is all and there is no "other",
the various perceptions rife
in the absence of Self-inquiry
and Self-abidance
are all seen as mere mistakes.

240. One forgets the Self
and thinks the body is oneself
and goes through innumerable births
and in the end remembers
and remains the Self.
Know this is only like
awaking from a dream
wherein one has wandered
all over the world.

241. Seeing this mind-projected world
in sheer delusion, then taking it as real,
and swerving from the Truth sublime
of one's own Being as pure Awareness,
one but proves oneself insane.

242. Destroying through discrimination
the basic error that I am the body,
an object, and rejecting it and the world
as mere mirages false, the Awareness that
surviving shines alone as Being, That am I.

243. When one now
deeming oneself the mind
and wandering lost amid phenomena,
wakes up from this dream-spectacle and
remerges in the Self and stands as That,
this is the inwardness of yoga true.

244. The universe out there appears when
scanned. But when not scanned,
it disappears. Turning away from this,
search keenly for the Self within the heart,
and think no more of birth.

245. Renouncing this phenomenal world which seems to, but does not exist, we gain the Self, the Awareness shining all unseen.

246. Seen through the eye of our true being which is awareness pure, supreme, what we call "birth" is but the folly of thinking that one is the body which forms a poor part of this entirely false phenomenal world.

247. Until the snake-illusion goes,
its ground, the real rope,
will not be recognized.
Until the world of false phenomena
disappears,
the Self, its ground,
will not shine clear.

248. Only when the world-illusion goes
does the blissful light of Self arrive.
Life lived in this bright, blissful light
is our true, natural life. Other ways
of life are full of trouble and fear.

249. Is there a greater folly
than the aching folly
of supposing that the Self,
the I of pure awareness
which does not see
this changing world at all,
is subject to some change?

250. Pure Being,
our Self-nature,
That alone exists eternally.

Apart from That,
all objects we perceive
are clusters of illusive appearances
that come and go,
while That,
unmoving and unchanged,
abides the same for ever.

SRI MURUGANAR
(251 – 261)

251. Absolute existence,
the pure sky of grace
free from the sorrow of 'I' and 'mine',
will be attained when,
in the mind that sees as the Self
and has died in that supreme reality,
the imaginary concepts of the world
and the physical body
have entirely ceased to be.

252. The eye of the Self,
consciousness,
alone constitutes true seeing.
That eye never perceives
anything at all.
If it be said that the eye
perceives anything whatsoever,
then that eye too,
like the thing it perceives,
is a mental creation.
It is not the true eye.

253. Know that the vision of the truth
we behold when we enter
and subside within the heart –
so that the treacherous ties
of worldly bondage
that attend the illusion of the body
are abolished –
is indeed
the gracious state of liberation.

254. In the heart,
the Self that exists as the eye of grace,
none of the worlds truly exist.

255. Ignorance will not be eradicated
except in those who,
through the power of Self-inquiry
conducted assiduously
within the heart,
have attained
the victorious absolute vision
in which the whole panoply
of manifestation is transcended,
being seen as a mere cinema show.

256. The infinite variety of false and treacherous modes of existence are merely brightly colored images appearing as if in a mirror. We must realize that the false and treacherous identification of the 'I' with the body is the seed from which these appearances arise to ensnare us, and we must reject it with disdain.

257. It is indeed pitiable to spurn, forfeit and lose the treasure that consists in dwelling thought-free within the Heart, on account of the vacillating mind that dwells upon the world-dream generated by the treacherous senses, taking it to be real.

258. The Self,
      revealed as our true nature
      within the heart
      through the power of Self-inquiry,
      is none other than the peerless reality
      of the Supreme, which alone remains
      after this worldly illusion
      has faded into nothingness.

259. That which is spoken of as the Life of life itself is the true life. That other 'life' is merely the body. That illusory knowledge mediated by the senses is nothing but delusion. The pure consciousness that underlies it alone is true consciousness.

260. The supreme reality – in which the noble nature of pure grace flourishes, and which merges with us so that all the many false appearances such as 'this birth' and 'the next birth' cease to exist – shines out as the truth-imbued and flawless 'I'.

261. If I am to affirm who I am,
          my true nature,
          I am the Self
          that knows nothing of
          the fleshly body,
          life, intelligence and mind,
          that is free of all darkness,
          the true 'I' that excels
          as pure consciousness.

SRI ANNAMALAI SWAMI
(262 – 270)

262. Mind and body are like the tongue and teeth in the mouth. They have to work in harmony with each other. The teeth do not fight with the tongue and bite it. Mind and body should combine in the same harmonious way. However, if we want to go beyond the body, beyond the mind, we have to understand and fully accept that all the information the senses provide is not real. Like the mirage that produces an illusory oasis in the desert, the senses create the impression that there is a real world in front of us that is being perceived by the mind. The apparent reality of the world is an illusion. It is merely a misperception. When the mind perceives a snake where in reality there is only a rope, this is clearly a case of the senses projecting an imaginary image unto a real substratum.

This, on a much larger scale, is how the unreal appearance of the world is projected by the mind and the senses unto the underlying reality of the Self. Once this happens, we see the superimposition, the unreal names and forms we have created, and we forget about the substratum, the reality that underlies them.

263. We think we live in a real, materially substantial world, and that our minds and bodies are real entities that move around in it. When the Self is seen and known, all these false ideas fade away and one is left with the knowledge: Self alone exists.

264. There are dream consequences for the bad acts committed in the dream, and while you still take the dream to be the reality, you will suffer the consequences of your bad behavior.

Do no evil and have no hate.
Have equanimity towards everything.

265. Since the Self is
     infinite and immaterial,
     what it 'sees' is
     infinite and immaterial.

266. Bad thoughts make bad dreams
     and good thoughts
     make good dreams,
     and if you have no thoughts
     you don't dream at all.

267. Your real state is the Self,
     and in that Self
     there is no body
     and no mind.

268. This life is all a dream, a dream
within a dream. We dream this world,
we dream that we die and take birth in
another body. And in this birth we dream
that we have dreams. All kinds
of pleasures and suffering alternate in
these dreams, but a moment comes when
waking up happens. In this moment,
which we call realizing the Self, there
is the understanding that all the births,
all the deaths, all the sufferings
and all the pleasures were unreal dreams
that have finally come to an end.

269. You are looking for satisfaction
      in the outside world
      because you think
      that all these objects
      you see in front of you are real.
      They are not.

270. If you abide as the Self,
      you will see the world as the Self.
      In fact, there will be no world at all.

SRI NISARGADATTA MAHARAJ
(271 – 316)

271. What do you know of me,
     when even my talk with you
     is in your world only?

272. Questioner:

Is your world full of things and people
as is mine?

Maharaj: No, it is full of myself.

273. The world you can perceive
     is a very small world indeed.
     And it is entirely private.
     Take it to be a dream
     and be done with it.

274. However long a life may be,
     it is but a moment
     and a dream.

275. In reality only the Ultimate is.
     The rest is a matter
     of name and form.
     And as long as you cling to the idea
     that only what has name
     and shape exists,
     the Supreme will appear to you
     non-existing.

     When you understand that
     names and shapes
     are hollow shells
     without any content whatsoever,
     and what is real
     is nameless and formless,
     pure energy of life
     and light of consciousness,
     you will be at peace –
     immersed in the deep silence
     of reality.

276. To take appearance for reality
     is a grievous sin
     and the cause of all calamities.

277. Within the prison of your world
     appears a man who tells you
     that the world of
     painful contradictions,
     which you have created,
     is neither continuous nor permanent
     and is based on a misapprehension.
     He pleads with you to get out of it,
     by the same way
     by which you got into it.
     You got into it
     by forgetting what you are
     and you will get out of it
     by knowing yourself as you are.

278. When you shall begin
     to question your dream,
     awakening will be not far away.

279. Your world is transient, changeful.
     My world is perfect, changeless.

280. In my world nothing happens.

281. Maharaj: My world is real,
     while yours is made of dreams.

Questioner: Yet we are talking.

Maharaj: The talk is in your world.
In mine – there is eternal silence.
My silence sings, my emptiness is full,
I lack nothing. You cannot know
my world until you are there.

282. Your mistake lies in your belief
that you are born. You were never born
nor will you ever die, but you believe that
you were born at a certain date and place
and that a particular body is your own.

283. It is in the nature of desire
     to prompt the mind to create a world
     for its fulfillment.

284. Desire can produce a universe;
     its powers are miraculous.

285.   In reality nothing ever happens.

286.   The only thing that can help
       is to wake up from the dream.

287.   Treating everything as a dream
       liberates.
       As long as you give reality to dreams,
       you are their slave.
       By imagining that you are born
       as so-and-so,
       you become a slave to the so-and-so.

288.   Only reality is, there is nothing else.
The three states of waking, dreaming and
sleeping are not me and I am not in them.

289.   The main point to grasp is that
you have projected unto yourself a world
of your own imagination,
based on memories,
on desires and fears,
and that you have imprisoned yourself
in it. Break the spell and be free.

290. Stop attributing names and shapes
to the essentially nameless and formless,
realize that every mode of perception
is subjective, that what is seen or heard,
touched or smelt, felt or thought,
expected or imagined,
is in the mind and not in reality,
and you will experience peace
and freedom from fear.

291. You cannot be rid of problems
without abandoning illusions.

292. Truth is permanent.
The real is changeless.
What changes is not real,
what is real does not change.

293. He who knows the state in which
there is neither the world nor the thought
of it, he is the Supreme Teacher.

294. In pure consciousness
nothing ever happens.

295. The real does not die,
     the unreal never lived.

296. You are neither the body nor in the
body – there is no such thing as body. You
have grievously misunderstood yourself;
to understand rightly – investigate.

297. My heart wants you awake. I see you
suffer in your dream and I know that you
must wake up to end your woes.
When you see your dream as dream,
you wake up. But in your dream itself
I am not interested. Enough for me
to know that you must wake up.

298. Do not be misled by
my eating and smoking,
reading and talking.
My mind is not here, my life is not here.
Your world,
of desires and their fulfillments,
of fears and their escapes, is definitely not
my world. I do not even perceive it.

299. Without imagination
there is no world.

300. The moment you allow
your imagination to spin,
it at once spins out a universe.
It is not at all as you imagine
and I am not bound
by your imaginings.

301. The intelligence and power
are all used up in your imagination.
It has absorbed you so completely
that you just cannot grasp
how far from reality
you have wandered.
No doubt imagination
is richly creative.
Universe within universe
are built on it.
Yet they are all in space and time,
past and future,
which just do not exist.

302. Maharaj: This body appears
in your mind; in my mind nothing is.

Questioner: Do you mean to say you are
quite unconscious of having a body?

Maharaj: On the contrary,
I am conscious of not having a body.

Questioner: I see you smoking!

Maharaj: Exactly so. You see me smoking.
Find out for yourself how did you come to
see me smoking, and you will easily realize
that it is your 'I-am-the-body' state of mind
that is responsible for this
'I-see-you-smoking' idea.

303. Questioner:
If all that passes has no being,
then the universe has no being either.

Maharaj: Who ever denies it?
Of course the universe has no being.

304. I am offering you
     exactly what you need – awakening.

305. Engrossed in a dream
     you have forgotten your true Self.

306. Nothing dies. The body is just
     imagined. There is no such thing.

307. There is no body, nor a world to
contain it; there is only a mental condition,
a dreamlike state, easy to dispel
by questioning its reality.

308. I am trying to wake you up,
     whatever your dream.

309. It is by your consent that the world
exists. Withdraw your belief in its reality
and it will dissolve like a dream.

310. Cease from looking for happiness
     and reality in a dream
     and you will wake up.

311. The world cannot give
what it does not have;
unreal to the core,
it is of no use for real happiness.
It cannot be otherwise.
We seek the real because
we are unhappy with the unreal.
Happiness is our real nature
and we shall never rest
until we find it.
But rarely we know where to seek it.
Once you have understood
that the world is
but a mistaken view of reality,
and is not what it appears to be,
you are free of its obsessions.
Only what is compatible
with your real being
can make you happy; and the world,
as you perceive it,
is its outright denial.

312. Do understand that what you think
to be the world is your own mind.

313. Once you have seen that you are
dreaming, you shall wake up. But you
do not see, because you want the dream
to continue. A day will come when
you will long for the ending of the dream,
with all your heart and mind,
and be willing to pay any price; the price
will be dispassion and detachment,
the loss of interest in the dream itself.

314. I do not need the world.
       Nor am I in one.

315. However great and complete
       is your world,
       it is self-contradictory and transitory
       and altogether illusory.

316. If you seek
       real happiness,
       unassailable and unchangeable,
       you must leave the world
       with its pains and pleasures
       behind you.

SRI VASISTHA
(317 – 511)

317. Neither freedom from sorrow nor
realization of one's real nature is possible
as long as the conviction does not arise
in one that the world-appearance is unreal.

318. All enjoyments in this world are
deluded, like the lunatic's enjoyment
of the taste of fruits reflected in a mirror.
All the hopes of man in this world
are consistently destroyed by time.

319. In this world there is nothing,
      high or low,
      that time does not destroy.

320. Neither the world of matter nor the
      modes of creation are truly real;
      yet the living and the dead
      think and feel they are real.
      Ignorance of this truth
      keeps up the appearance.

321. As long as the highest wisdom
does not dawn in the heart, the person
revolves in this wheel of birth and death.

322. The materiality of the creation is like
the castle in the air, an illusory projection
of one's own mind – imaginary.

323. When this notion of the object
        is firmly rejected
        and removed from the subject,
        then consciousness alone exists
        without even an apparent
        or potential objectivity.

324. The wrong notion that
this world is real has become deep rooted
on account of persistent wrong thinking.

325. What is known as liberation is indeed
        the absolute itself, which alone is.
        That which is perceived here as 'I',
        'you' etc., only seems to be,
        for it has never been created.

326. In truth, this world does not arise
from the absolute nor does it merge in it.
The absolute alone exists now and for ever.

327. All this is mere imagination or
thought. Even now nothing has ever been
created; the pure infinite space alone exists.

328. Cosmic consciousness
        alone exists
        now and ever;
        in it are no worlds,
        no created beings.

329. Even as
an unreal nightmare produces real results,
this world seems to give rise
to a sense of reality in a state of ignorance.
When true wisdom arises,
this unreality vanishes.

330. Changes in the unchanging
        are imagined
            by ignorant and deluded people.

331. This world and this creation
       is nothing but memory, dream:
       distance, measures of time
       like a moment and an age,
       all these are hallucinations.

332. Liberation is the realization of the
total non-existence of the universe as such.
This is different from a mere denial of
the existence of the ego and the universe!
The latter is only half-knowledge.

333. In dream,
the dream-body appears to be real;
but when there is an awakening to the fact
of dream, the reality of that body vanishes.
Even so, the physical body
which is sustained by memory
and latent tendencies is seen to be unreal
when they are seen to be unreal.

334. There is no universe,
       no distance,
       no barriers.

335. It is the nature of appearance to
appear to be real, even though it is unreal.

336. In the mind of the deluded,
the unreal manifests itself;
and when the delusion has been dispelled
there is no longer an ignorant fancy. This
fanciful conviction that the unreal is real
is deep-rooted by repeated imagination.

337. The physical body is only the creation
       of one's ignorant fancy, not real.

338. No creation takes place
       in the Supreme Being
       or the infinite consciousness;
       and the infinite consciousness
       is not involved in the creation.

339. When there is notion of creation,
       the creation seems to be:
       and when, through self-effort,
       there is understanding
       of non-creation, there is no world.

340. Even as liquor is able to make one see
all sorts of phantasms in the empty sky,
mind is able to make one see diversity
in unity. Even as a drunkard sees
a tree moving, the ignorant one
sees movement in this world.

341. When the mind entertains notions of
objects, there is agitation or movement
in the mind; and when there are no objects
or ideas, then there is no movement
of thought in the mind. When there is
movement, the world appears to be;
when there is no movement,
there is cessation of world-appearance.

342. In truth,
        there is no creation,
        and hence no division at all.

343. When the world
is assumed to be real, the Self is not seen:
but when this assumption is discarded,
consciousness is realized.

344. The seer alone is real,
the object being hallucination.

345. When Self-knowledge arises
and the object ceases to be,
the seer is realized as the sole reality.

346. It is the mind
that makes things appear here.
It brings about the appearance
of the body, etc.,
naught else is aware of the body.

347. The infinite consciousness alone IS.

348. Some arrive at this understanding
soon, others after a very long time.

349. When we inquire into
the nature of the mind,
all the created objects or all appearances
are seen to be its creations;
only the infinite consciousness remains
as uncreated by the mind.

350. The enlightened one knows
that there is only one reality –
the infinite consciousness.

351. This world is nothing
but pure hallucination.

352. The mind veils
the real nature of the Self
and creates an illusory appearance
with many branches,
flowers and fruits.
Destroy this illusion by wisdom
and rest in peace.

353. The seed of this world-appearance
is ignorance.

354. It is only the limitation of thought
that perceives the world-appearance.
This world-appearance is delusion:
it is better not to let
the very thought of it
arise again in the mind.

355. It is only in a state of ignorance that the mind dreams of the world-appearance, not when it is awake or enlightened.

356. Such indeed is the nature of this utter ignorance, this delusion, and this world-process: without real existence there is this illusory notion of egotism. This egotism does not exist in the infinite Self. In the infinite Self there is no creator, no creation, no worlds, no heaven, no humans, no demons, no bodies, no elements, no time.

357. There is no creation.
      The infinite has never abandoned
      its infinity.
      THAT has never become this.

358. The power of nescience is capable
      of creating a total confusion
      between the real and the unreal.

359. Nescience and the Self
      cannot have any relationship.

360. Thought alone creates
all these divisions and illusions.
When it ceases, creation ceases.

361. Only as long as the delusion
of this world-appearance lasts
is there this existence of the world
as an object of perception.

362. This world-appearance
is experienced only like a day-dream;
it is essentially unreal.

363. There is no cause and effect relation
between the Supreme Being
and the universe.

364. The world is not seen in
the supreme non-dual consciousness.

365. Mind alone by its thinking faculty
conjures up what is known
as the body: no body is seen
where the mind does not function!

366. It is the mind that creates the body
with all its limbs.
Mind itself is both the sentient
and the insentient beings;
all this endless diversity
is nothing but mind.

367. It is the mind that 'creates' the body
by mere thoughts.

368. The ignorant man with a gross
physical vision sees the physical body
as different from
and independent of the mind.

369. It is indeed true to say
that there are no waves in the ocean;
the ocean alone exists.

370. The physical body is nothing
but the fruit of the fancy of the mind;
the physical body
is not an existential fact
independent of the mind.

371. This world exists only in appearance
   or imagination
   and not because one sees
   the material substances.
   It is like a long dream
   or a juggler's trick.

372. Each individual sees only those
objects which are rooted in his own mind.
When the ideas in the mind do not bear
fruits, there is a change in the mind;
there follows a succession of births
to suit these psychological changes.

It is this psychological connection that
creates the conviction in the reality of birth
and death and in the reality of the body.
When this conviction is given up,
there is the cessation of embodiment.

373. The notions of 'I' and 'the world'
   are but shadows,
   not truth.

374. He sees the truth who sees the body
     as a product of
     deluded understanding
     and as the fountain-source
     of misfortune;
     and who knows that the body
     is not the Self.

375. He sees the truth
     who is not deluded into thinking
     that he is the body
     which is subject to illness,
     fear, agitation, old age and death.

376. He sees the truth who knows that
     the Self alone exists
     and that there is no substance
     to objectivity.

377. Mind alone is this universe.

378. Consciousness
       reflecting in consciousness
       shines as consciousness
       and exists as consciousness;
       yet, to one who is ignorant,
       though considering oneself
       as wise and rational,
       there arises the notion
       that there has come into being
       and there exists something
       other than this consciousness.

379. The mind alone is this world-
appearance, this world appearance
has arisen in it and it rests in the mind.
When the objects as well as the
experiencing mind have become tranquil,
consciousness alone remains.

380. There is no world in reality.

381. All this creation takes place only as
       in a dream. This creation is not real;
       it merely appears to be so.

382. These universes arise and vanish
again and again. But these are different
from the one infinite consciousness.

383. All this is unreal, like the creations
seen in a dream. Hence the question:
"How did all this arise in the one infinite
consciousness?" is immature and childish.
The creation appears to take place
on account of the intentions of the mind.

384. This creation is nothing but the
creation of the mind: this is the truth;
the rest is but a fanciful description.

385. The repetition
(creation and dissolution)
of infinite number of universes,
with the infinite variety of creators
in them,
is nothing but the fanciful perception
of the ignorant and the deluded.

386. Your birth is unreal.

387. The Self is devoid of the senses.

388. That alone
can be regarded as the truth
which has always been
and which will always be.

389. Mind alone is the seed for this
delusion of world-appearance;
it is the mind that gives rise
to the false sense of "I" and "mine."

390. Nothing in this world
is truly enduring.

391. What you see as the world
is only an illusory appearance.

392. The Self is real,
birth and death are imaginary.

393. I am the unborn
in whom the world-appearance
has vanished.

394. It is only in the eyes of the ignorant
that even your form exists.

395. This cosmic illusion
leads the unwary mind
into endless difficulties.

396. When one is firmly established
in Self-knowledge,
which is infinite,
unlimited and unconditioned,
then the delusion or ignorance
that gave rise to world-appearance
comes to an end.

397. The sun and the worlds
become non-objects of perception
to them who have gone beyond
the realm of objective perception
and knowledge.

398. The ignorant man does not realize
the unreality of the objects
because he has not realized the reality.

399. When you have gained Self-
knowledge and when your consciousness
has infinitely expanded, your mind no
longer falls into the cesspool of this world.

400. There is no way
        other than Self-knowledge
        for the cutting asunder of bondage
        and for crossing this ocean of illusion.

401. The supreme Self has no relationship
        with this world-appearance.

402. The ignorant person accepts as real
whatever he sees in this world;
not so the wise one. Even as a piece of
wood and water in which it is reflected
have no real relationship, the body
and the Self have no real relationship.

403. This universe
        has been conjured up in empty space
        merely by mental conditioning:
        it is not a reality.

404. There is no duality;
there are no bodies and therefore
there are no relationships
among them.

405. Be not deluded.
Abandon false perception
and behold the truth.

406. When the mind abandons
the movement of thought,
the appearance of the world-illusion
ceases.

407. Caught up in his own conditioning,
whatever the person sees, he thinks that to
be real and gets deluded. And on account
of the intensity of the conditioning
and the fancy, he discards his own nature
and perceives only the world-illusion.

408. This entire creation
is pervaded by ignorance
which sustains it.

409. Birth and childhood lead to youth;
youth leads to old age;
and old age ends in death – and
all these are repeatedly experienced
by the ignorant.

410. Nothing has really become
physical or material.

411. That which has a beginning
has an end. When all things
that have a beginning
are ruled out,
what remains is the truth
which is the cessation of ignorance.

412. This house known as the body has
not been made by anyone in fact! It is only
an appearance, like the two moons seen by
one suffering from diplopia. The moon is
really only one; the duality is an optical
illusion. The body is experienced to exist
only when the notion of a physical body
prevails in the mind; it is unreal.

413. There are thousands of such bodies
which have been brought into being
by your thought-force.

414. By continually entertaining notions
such as "This is it.", "This is mine."
and "This is my world."
such notions assume the appearance
of substantiality.
The permanency of the world
is also an illusion:
in the dream-state
what is really a brief moment
is experienced by the dreamer
as a lifetime. In a mirage
only the illusory "water" is seen
and not the substratum:
even so, in a state of ignorance
one sees only
the illusory world-appearance
but not the substratum.
However,
when one has shed that ignorance,
the illusory appearance vanishes.

415. For your spiritual awakening
I declare again and again:
this world-appearance is like a long dream.
Wake up, wake up.
Behold the Self which shines like a sun.

416. You have nothing to do with birth,
sorrow, sin and delusion. Abandon
all these notions and rest in the Self.

417. The infinite consciousness
        alone exists, naught else exists.

418. Consciousness does not
        truly undergo any modification
        nor does it become impure.

419. Since that omnipresent infinite
consciousness alone is present at all times,
diversity is absurd and impossible.

420. The reality is beginningless and
        endless and it is not even reflected
        in anything: that is the reality.

421. Nothing is created in or by
     cosmic consciousness
     for it remains unchanged
     and unmodified.

422. The mountain seen in a dream only
     appears to exist in time and space.
     It does not occupy any space
     nor does it take time to appear
     and disappear.
     Even so is the case with the world.

423. This world-illusion
     has arisen
     because of the movement of thought
     in the mind;
     when that ceases
     the illusion will cease, too,
     and the mind becomes no-mind.

424. The unreal alone dies
     and it is the unreal
     that is born again
     apparently in another body.

425. Wherever the world is seen,
that is but an illusory
world-appearance.
This illusion, and therefore bondage,
is sustained by
psychological conditioning.
Such conditioning is bondage
and its abandonment is freedom.

426. Because the "world"
is in fact only an appearance,
it is in reality emptiness,
void and unreal.

427. The world-appearance is illusory.

428. That which is born of the unreal
must be unreal, too.

Hence,
though this world appears to be real,
as it is born of the unreal concept,
it should be firmly rejected.

429. Just as one who is immersed in the dream sees the dream as utterly real, one who is immersed in this creation thinks that it is utterly real. Just as one goes from one dream to another, one goes from one delusion to another delusion and thus experiences this world as utterly real.

430. It is on account of ignorance that this long-dream world-appearance appears to be real.

431. It is by Self-knowledge that the unreality of the concepts concerning worldly objects is realized.

432. Consciousness does not undergo any change: the only apparent change is the illusory appearance which is illusory and therefore not real!

433. The external phenomena are utterly useless.

434. There is but one consciousness
which is pure, invisible,
the subtlest of the subtle, tranquil,
which is neither the world nor its activities.

435. There is no such thing as creation.
You are neither the doer of actions nor the
enjoyer of experiences. You are the all,
ever at peace, unborn and perfect.

436. The world has no basis at all.

437. It is the movement of thought
that appears as this world.

438. This world-appearance
is like a dream.

439. On the awakening
of the inner intelligence,
the world-perception ceases and
there arises psychological freedom
or non-attachment.
That is known as emancipation.

440. There is nothing other than the Self.

441. What appears to be the world
is the expansion of one's own notions
or thoughts.

442. It is only when the eyes
are blinded by ignorance
that one perceives
the world of diversity.

443. Creation has not taken place.
It is but an appearance
like the mirage.

444. You are a knower.
Whether you know something
or do not,
remain free from doubt.
When you realize that you are
the unborn, infinite consciousness,
then all ignorance
and foolishness cease
and this world-appearance ceases.

445. All these worlds, etc. come into being and cease to be as notions and nothing more. Consciousness does not undergo any change in all these. In consciousness there is no experience of pleasure or pain, nor does a notion arise in it as "This I am."

446. There is the unreal experience
of this world
and what is known as
the other-world,
though all these are false.

447. He who does not abandon
his confirmed conviction
in the existence of diversity
is not abandoned by sorrow.

448. When one falls into
this illusion of world-appearance,
he is at once preyed upon
by countless other illusions
which arise in the original illusion.

449. If you close your eyes, the vision of
the external world is blotted out:
if you remove the notion of the world
from your consciousness,
pure consciousness alone exists.

450. The world and the "I" exist only as
notions, not as fact nor as reality.

451. Creation, world,
movement of consciousness, etc.
are mere words without substance.
When such ideas are abandoned,
the "world" and the "I" cease to be
and consciousness alone exists,
pure and immutable.

This unconditioned consciousness
alone is, naught else is –
not even the nature of
diverse objects here.

452. The illusory appearance of objects
is of no practical use.

453. When you affirm
the reality of the illusory appearance,
you invite unhappiness;
when its unreality is realized
there is great happiness.

454. The notion of the reality
of the objects of this world
arises only in ignorance.

455. Confusion or delusion is unreal
and the unreal does not exist.

456. In their mind,
my body seems to be real;
but to my illumined intelligence,
their physical existence is unreal,
as it is to a sleeping person.

457. When one is fully established
in the Self,
then this world-appearance ceases
like dream during deep sleep.

458. As surely as it is a certainty that where there is sunlight there is illumination, where there is experience of the essencelessness of the worldly objects, there occurs spiritual awakening.

459. The world-appearance
arises in ignorance
and wisdom puts an end to it.

460. When what exists is realized as it is,
the world-appearance ceases.

461. Do not be deluded
by this illusory world-appearance.

462. To the man of Self-knowledge
what the ignorant man thinks real
(time, space, matter, etc.)
are non-existent.

463. In the eyes of the wise man
there is no world.

464. That is known as the attainment of
the highest in which one abandons the
notions of the existence of objects and in
which one rests in one's own pure Self.
When all divisions are given up,
the indivisible alone remains.
It is pure, one, beginningless and endless.

465. When wisdom
   is strengthened and confirmed, and
   when the impurity of conditioning
   is washed away,
   the holy one shines
   with an extraordinary radiance.
   Both the inner notion and
   the external perception of the world
   cease for him.

466. Behold the entire universe
   composed of you, I, mountains,
   gods and demons, etc.
   as you would behold
   the creations and the happenings
   of a dream.

467. I saw many universes and their
diversity aroused my curiosity.
I wanted to roam more and more to see the
magnitude of creation. After some time,
I abandoned that idea knowing that it was
delusion and remained established in
the infinite consciousness.
Instantly, all this perception of diversity
vanished from my sight.
There was the pure consciousness,
nothing else. This is the truth:
all else is imagination, notion, delusion
or illusory perception.

468. There is no such thing
        as earth or matter.

469. Duality or diversity is false:
        the one mass
        of infinite consciousness
        alone is real.

470. There is no such thing as the world.

471. This body is but pure void,
it seems to exist on account of
the mental conditioning.
When the latter ceases,
the body ceases to be seen or experienced,
just as the dream-object is not experienced
on waking up.

472. Neither the subtle body nor the gross
body is seen even in the waking state
when the mental conditioning ceases.

473. This universe has no form,
no body,
no materiality,
though it seems to have a form.

474. You imagine that I have a body.
It is on account of this notion
existing in you
that I produce this sound
known as speech.
You hear it even as a sleeping person
hears sounds in his dream.

475. The diversity perceived in a dream
does not create a diversity in the dreamer;
even so the notion of a creation does not
create a division in consciousness.
Consciousness alone is, no creation;
the dream-mountain is the dreamer,
not a mountain.

476. The world is an appearance
        and not existence.

477. What is unreal is unreal,
        even if it has been experienced
        for a long time by all.

478. Neither in the waking state
        or in dream is there a real world.

479. When sleep has ceased, the world-
appearance rises; when that ceases there is
pure consciousness. That "nothing"
which remains after everything
has been negated as "not this, not this"
is pure consciousness.

480. In the vision
          of the knowers of the truth,
          there is nothing other than
          the pure and infinite consciousness,
          and the objective universe
          is completely and totally
          non-existent.

481. Besides this there are other universes
of which I have not told you. For of what
use is investigation into the nature of the
world and others which are but of the
nature of a dream; wise men do not waste
their time talking about useless things.

482. When Self-knowledge arises,
          the illusory notion
          of a world-existence
          vanishes.

483. Though the body-notion is unreal
          it is experienced as if it were real,
          just like the dream-object.

484. Even the original creation is like a dream. It is but an illusory appearance. Though devoid of earth, and all the rest of it, it appears to have earth, etc.

485. The original dreamlike creation of the world and also the dream that we experience now are both unreal.

486. There is no death,
        and by the same token
        there is no birth either.

487. Realize that this world-appearance with all its contradictions is nothing more than appearance which is non-existent.

488. That which is firmly believed to exist is experienced by that person physically, for the body is only mind.

489. Just as some people remember
        their dreams, some people
        also remember their past existences.

490. Consciousness is infinite peace
     which exists forever unmodified.

491. It is good to remind yourself
     that all this is but a long dream.

492. Just as the dream-mountain
     is realized as pure void
     when the dreamer wakes up,
     even so are all these forms
     realized to be non-existent
     when one is enlightened.

493. When the wise one realizes
     that this world is like a dream-city,
     his hopes are not centered in it.

494. Only when it is realized
     that there is no creation at all
     does real Self-knowledge arise
     which leads to liberation.
     Such liberation is unending,
     infinite and unconditioned.

495. The objective universe is delusion
or illusion; it does not disappear
except through persistent practice.

496. Whatever objects are perceived in this
world are the mind only, even as
the dream-objects are the mind only.

497. In this subtle body there arise the
thoughts or concepts of physical bodies
and their component parts, concepts of
birth, activity, etc., concepts of time, space,
sequence, etc., as also concepts of old age,
death, virtue and defect, knowledge, etc.
Having conjured up these concepts, the
subtle body itself experiences the objective
universe composed of the five elements as
if it existed in reality. But all this
is surely illusory, like dream-objects
and dream-experiences.

498. When there is the notion of reality
in unreal phenomena,
there is bondage.

499. Something which is unreal
does not arise in the real.

500. There is no illusion in the infinite.

501. This illusion of world-appearance
vanishes when one is awakened and
enlightened. Then one realizes that it has
never been, it is not and it will never be.

502. The unreal does not exist at all
at any time.

503. When dream is realized as dream,
the false notion vanishes.
Awareness drops its object and
rests in the infinite consciousness.

504. This world has arisen like a dream.

505. Nothing,
not even this body,
has ever been created.

506. Like a frog in the blind well,
foolish and ignorant people
base their understanding
on the experience of the moment and, on
account of their perverse understanding,
they are deluded into thinking
that the body alone
is the source of experience or awareness.

507. What you have called the body
    does not exist in the eyes of the sage.

508. There is no "dream"
    in the infinite consciousness.
    There is neither a body
    nor a dream in it.

509. Though this universe
    seems to have existed for a long time
    and though it seems to be a
    functional reality, still it is pure void
    and it is no more real
    than an imaginary city.

510. Nothing exists here
and therefore
there are no concepts of objects;
there is nothing other than the Self
and the Self
does not conceive of an object.

511. It is only as long
as you are not fully enlightened
that you experience
apparent diversity.

SRI SANKARA
(512 – 524)

512. Where has the world gone?
Who has removed it,
or where has it disappeared to?
I saw it only just now,
and now it is not there.

513. The products of natural causation,
from the idea of doership down to
the body itself and all its senses, are
also unreal in view of the way they
are changing every moment, while
one's true nature itself never changes.

514. Give up identification
with this mass of flesh
as well as with what thinks it a mass.
Both are intellectual imaginations.
Recognize your true Self
as undifferentiated awareness,
unaffected by time, past, present
or future, and enter Peace.

515. The living organism, which is thought to belong to oneself through its identification with the intellect, does not really exist. On the other hand, the true Self is quite distinct from it, and the identification of oneself with the intellect is due to misunderstanding.

516. The mistaken imagination of illusion is not a reality.

517. As the darkness, that is its opposite, is melted away in the radiance of the sun, so, indeed, all things visible are melted away in the Eternal.

518. Reaching bodiless purity, mere Being, partless, the being of the Eternal, the sage returns to this world no more.

519. I see not, nor hear, nor know aught of this world; for I bear the mark of the Self, whose form is being and bliss.

520. The belief in this world
is built up of unreality.

521. The world no longer is,
whether past, present, or to come,
after awakening to the supreme
reality, in the real Self, the Eternal,
from all wavering free.

522. All changing forms in nature
beginning with personality and ending
with the body, and all sensual objects;
these are unreal, because subject to change
every moment; but the Self never changes.

523. There is no freedom for him who is
full of attachment to the body
and its like; for him who is free,
there is no wish
for the body and its like;
the dreamer is not awake,
he who is awake dreams not;
for these things are the opposites
of each other.

524. In as much as all this world,
     body and organs,
     vital breath and personality
     are all unreal,
     in so much
     THOU ART THAT,
     the restful,
     the stainless,
     secondless Eternal,
     the supreme.

Please use the contact form at seeseer.com to let us know if reading the book Everything is an Illusion was a good experience for you.

The six books in the Self Realization Series are:

1.   *Self Awareness Practice Instructions.*

The most direct and rapid means to Self Realization goes by various names including:

A.   *Self Inquiry.*
B.   *Self Abidance.*
C.   *Self Attention.*
D.   *Self Awareness.*
E.   *Abiding as Awareness.*
F.   *Awareness of Awareness.*
G.   *Awareness Aware of Itself.*
H.   *Awareness Watching Awareness.*

The book Self Awareness Practice Instructions contains all of the quotes in Chapter (Step) Seven from the book The Seven Steps to Awakening and also both Chapter Seven: Practice Instructions for the Awareness Watching Awareness Method and Chapter Eight: Further Clarification of the Awareness Watching Awareness Method from the book The Most Direct Means to Eternal Bliss.

2.   *The Desire for Liberation.*

The awakening of the extremely intense desire for Liberation is the most important aid to Self Realization. The book The Desire for Liberation contains all of the quotes in Chapter (Step) Four from the book The Seven Steps to Awakening and both Chapter Four: The Desire for Liberation and Chapter Five: How to Awaken the Extremely Intense Desire for Liberation from the book The Most Direct Means to Eternal Bliss.

3.	*The False self.*

The false self goes by many different names including:

A.	*Ego.*
B.	*Mind.*
C.	*Thinking*
D.	*A bundle of thoughts*
E.	*The impostor self.*

The book The False self contains all of the quotes in Chapter (Step) Three from the book The Seven Steps to Awakening. It also contains the contents of Chapter One: The Impostor, Chapter Two: The Impostor's Tricks and Chapter Three: The Impostor's Tools from the book The Most Direct Means to Eternal Bliss.

4.	*Inspiration and Encouragement*
	on the Path to Self Realization.

This collection of quotes is for the purpose of inspiring, encouraging and motivating those who are seeking Self Realization.

That includes being inspired, encouraged and motivated to:

A. *Make and maintain the decision to bring the impostor self to its final end and thus to remain eternally as your true Self which is Absolutely Perfect Infinite-Awareness-Love-Bliss that has never experienced any sorrow or suffering in all of eternity.*

B. *Drop all of your unnecessary activities and use all of the free time thus created to practice the most direct and rapid means leading to Self Realization. The Seven Sages placed tremendous emphasis on the importance of practice.*

The more times you read these quotes the better. Read all of these quotes every day, or at least be sure to read them every time you feel the need to be inspired, encouraged or motivated to get back on track in one-pointedness towards your spiritual goal and spiritual practice. The quotes in this book are the same as the quotes in Chapter (Step) Five from the book The Seven Steps to Awakening.

5.   Everything is an Illusion.

What is helpful about reading these types of quotes is that the more you can realize that everything is an illusion the better you can ignore everything and turn inward. One of the most significant aspects to this collection of quotes by the Sages is that in addition to pointing out that everything is a dreamlike illusion, they also point out in many of their quotes that upon Self Realization everything disappears. This book contains all of the quotes in Chapter (Step) Two from the book The Seven Steps to Awakening.

6.   How Not to Get Lost in Concepts.

A mistake made by almost everyone who studies the Direct Path Teachings is that instead of using the teachings as practice instructions they become lost in spiritual concepts. Most of those people never correct that mistake and at the end of their physical life they are still lost in a maze of concepts without having realized the Self. This book contains all of the quotes in Chapter (Step) One from the book The Seven Steps to Awakening.

For more information about these books go to:

www.seeseer.com

CPSIA information can be obtained at www.ICGtesting.com
Printed in the USA
BVOW07s1809260713

326831BV00003B/886/P